LDS SNIGGLES

BRAD WILCOX & CLARK SMITH

Illustrated by Brent Watts

George &
Dett :
Thanks for your
support and friendship
Best wishes
Brad Wilcox

Bookcraft
Salt Lake City, Utah

To our friends in the BYU Outreach Program
and to everyone else who has noticed
humorous aspects of life in the Church
and not known what to call them

Copyright © 1987 by Bookcraft, Inc.
Library of Congress Catalog Card Number: 87-71586
ISBN 0-88494-634-7
First Printing, 1987
Second Printing, 1988

Printed in the United States of America

ACKNOWLEDGMENTS

We express appreciation to the contributors listed, whose creative efforts form a large part of this book. We are grateful too to Craig Bradley for bringing the two of us together; to Cory Maxwell and Jana Erickson for getting this idea off the ground; and, as always, to George Bickerstaff and Chloe Vroman for encouraging us to write.

CONTRIBUTORS

Margaret and Matt Balkman, Katie and Reed Blake, Charles Bradshaw, Danny Bradshaw, Janet and Merrill Bradshaw, John Bytheway, Cray Carlsen, Shirley Condie, Joe Crawford, Shauna and Blair Davies, Darren Davis, Edgemont sixth graders, Troy Eickler, Darren Fortie, Mark Gunnell, Mary Lois and Earl Leroy Gunnell, Robin and Steve Gunnell, Joel Halquist, Karen Maxwell, Anne and John Moss, Gary Nelson, Lois Satler, Marie and C. Dennis Smith, Mark Smith, Mike Smith, Pam and Jon Tucker, Jim Usevitch, Cheryl and Chris Wilcox, Debi Wilcox, Margo and Wayne Wilcox, Moana and Roger Wilcox, Val and Ray Wilcox.

OFFICIAL LDS SNIGGLES ENTRIES

Send your LDS Sniggles that are every bit as clever as any in this book to:

LDS Sniggles
2835 Rio Claro Drive
Hacienda Heights, CA 91745

A LAURELM
(ah 'law ruhlm)

The growing anxiety felt by Laurels who have not yet been asked out.

A T & TIGUED
('ay 'tee uhn 'teegd)

A condition of the dialing finger, usually suffered by executive secretaries.

AMU-SING
(uh 'myu sing)

When the opening song of the tenth meeting you have attended on a given Sunday is "There Is an Hour of Peace and Rest."

AREALAGRIPPA
(uh 'reel uh 'grip uh)

An Italian missionary's handshake.

ARISTATTLE
('ayr i 'statl)

A ward member who attempts to answer every question the Gospel Doctrine teacher asks.

ASHOESTICS
(uh 'shoo stiks)

The startling sound of shoes clomping on the floor of the cultural hall during sacrament meeting. (*See also* Tiptowaddle.)

BANNEDAGE
('band ayj)

Wounded feeling experienced by deacons or Beehives when a multistake dance is planned two weeks before his or her fourteenth birthday.

BASKETCASE
('bas ket 'kays)

The elder who won't miss a ward basketball game but who can never quite find time to go home teaching.

BAYER PRAYER
('bayr 'prayr)

The act of disguising the blessing on food eaten in a public place by bringing the hands to the forehead as though easing a headache.

BEARBYSITTERS
('bayr bee sit uhrz)

The worn, stuffed teddies in the nursery toy box that every kid in the ward has grown up with.

BEEHIVIOR
(bee 'hiyv yohr)

Adolescent conduct that often appears as young women go to girls camp.

BENEVACUATION
('ben ee 'vak yu 'ay shun)

The act of leaving large church gatherings before the closing prayer.

BEWELDERED
(bee 'wel durhd)

An investigator's confusion when he finds that all missionaries have the same first name.

BISHOPDERMUS
('bish uhp 'duhr muhs)

The portion of skin revealed between the bottom of a bishop's pants and the top of his socks when he crosses his legs while sitting on the stand.

BISHOPNOIA
('bish uhp 'noy uh)

Paranoia that often strikes when the bishop calls and asks you to meet with him in his office.

BLESSABYE
('bles uh by)

Rhythmic bouncing arm movement generated by priesthood holders while blessing a baby. (*See also* Weewahs.)

BLESSINCOMES
('bles in cuhmz)

Little added blessings that seem to show up from nowhere for full-tithe payers.

BLESSTURE
('bles chuhr)

A proud father's showing off his baby to the congregation after having given it a name and a blessing.

BLUFFNOD
('bluhf 'nawd)

A gesture used by new missionaries in foreign countries when they are pretending to understand what is going on.

BOYANCY
('boy uhn see)

The ability to stay afloat for more than six months in any Scout calling.

BULL-DOZED
('buhl dohzd)

The feeling you get when you have to sit through an entire lesson taught by an unprepared teacher.

CELECSTACY
(suh 'lek stuh see)

The feeling enjoyed by parents of the bride and groom at a temple wedding.

CHAIRUBUMP
('chayr yu 'buhmp)

The sound of folding chairs knocking against classroom walls as students lean back on them.

CHAPERUINED
('shap uh 'roo uhnd)

The feeling experienced by adult supervisors after a weekend at youth conference. (Not to be confused with Chaperooned: The feeling of a lone adult when no one else shows up to supervise a youth dance.)

CHAREDIBLES
('chayr 'ed uh buhlz)

Holiday tidbits received from visiting teachers.

CHEERI-OH-OH
('cheer ee 'oh oh)

The look a child gives his parents after he has spilled Cheerios for the tenth time during sacrament meeting.

CINEMIZED
('sin uh myzd)

When you find you can recite every word of dialogue in one of the frequently seen Church films.

CLERKULATIONS
('kluhrk yu 'lay shuhnz)

Little marks clerks make on hand-held cards in order to keep track of their count as they go up and down the aisles.

CLOCKSELERATION
(klawk 'sel uhr 'ay shun)

The magical speeding up of the minute hand during the last half hour before you need to leave for church.

COMMERCELATION
(kuhm 'uhrs ee 'lay shun)

The sudden thrill experienced when an LDS "commercial" comes on TV or radio.

CONGROLENCES
(kawn 'groh luhn suhz)

Expressions of enthusiasm (and sympathy) given to the wife of a newly called bishop.

CONTENTIMENT
('kuhn 'tent uh ment)

The feeling enjoyed by parents at seminary graduation.

DECONNED
('dee kawnd)

When priests and Laurels volunteer deacons to do a service project.

DIRACTOR
(duh 'rak tuhr)

The conductor who directs a five-member ward choir using dramatic gestures on a Tabernacle Choir scale.

DISDRESS
(dis 'dres)

The emotional response of a girl who wears a new dress to a Church activity, only to find two other Laurels wearing the same dress.

DISPEWTED
(dis 'pyu tuhd)

Displacement felt by an established family in the ward when a new family sits on the very bench they always use.

DOORWARS
('dohr wohrz)

Tugs on the chapel doors as the usher holds them closed during a prayer or the sacrament service.

DOUBTFOUL
('dowt 'fowl)

The look on a church referee's face when he doesn't know what to call.

DOYAKNOW
('doo yuh 'noh)

Your immediate reaction upon learning that the person you are talking to has served in the same mission as you.

DOZNOTES
('dohz 'nohts)

Organ or piano sounds made during a meeting when the accompanist accidently touches the keyboard.

EARLY WORM
('uhr lee 'wuhrm)

The visiting teacher who likes to stop by just after dropping off her car pool at early morning seminary.

ELUSIVICITY
(ee 'loo si 'vi si tee)

The ability of some members to move just before their membership records arrive.

EMOTECONTROL
(ee 'moht cuhn 'trohl)

The struggle to hold back tears at baptisms and sealings.

EMPRAYER-ESSMENT
(em 'prayr uhs muhnt)

When home teachers pray a blessing on your family but cannot remember your names.

ENDSIGNS
('end synz)

Banners taken to airports or hung at home to welcome returning missionaries.

ENSIGNTIQUES
('en syn 'teeks)

Old copies of rarely used Church magazines that accumulate in the meetinghouse library.

ETERNI-TIES
(ee 'tuhrn uh 'tyz)

Ties that get passed from Elder to Elder, never leaving the mission.

EVENTTIDE
(ee 'vent tyd)

The swell in attendance due to a missionary farewell, baby blessing, or confirmation.

EVIDENTS
('ev uh 'dents)

Telling indentations on the foreheads of teenage boys who nap with their heads on the benches in front of them during sacrament meeting. (*See also* Slurch.)

F.H.E. TV
('ef 'aych 'ee 'tee 'vee)

When Dad wants to watch a TV program on Monday night, so he declares it to be the family night activity.

FAKEBAKE
('fayk 'bayk)

The act of going to the bakery for the "homemade" apple pie you volunteered to make for a ward dinner.

FAMISHTERICAL
('fam ish 'tayr uh kuhl)

The condition of being so hungry in church on fast day that even a little child's Fruit Loops look tempting.

FARK
(fahrk)

Utensil used at Utah ward dinners to eat the carn.

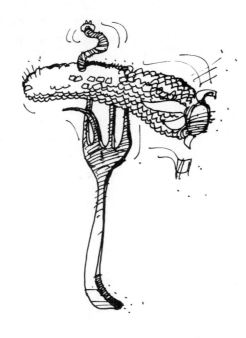

FASTNESIA
(fast 'nee zee uh)

Failure of memory that occurs as members lean over to take drinks from the church drinking fountain on the first Sunday of the month.

FELLOWSLIPPING
('fel oh 'slip ing)

When the congregation welcomes new members into the ward, and the new members are not there to stand as their names are called.

FLOCK BLOCK
('flawk 'blawk)

A gathering of chattering ward members in the middle of the church hallway.

FLUKECAKES
('flook 'kayks)

Holiday treats that travel around the ward as recipients change name tags and pass them on.

FORGOODNESS-BAKE
(for 'good nuhs 'bayk)

The goodie you volunteer to make for a Church fund-raiser and end up buying back yourself.

FOUNTOLOGIST
(foun 'tawl uh jist)

A parent who has mastered the art of holding up a thirsty child, pushing the button on the drinking fountain, and keeping his own clothes dry at least five times during every sacrament meeting. (*See also* Thirstafeliac.)

GEOGRIEFY
(jee 'aw gree fee)

The constant checking of the mailbox for an expected mission call.

GIGGLAFIT
('gig luh fit)

Trying to control those uncontrollable giggles at church.

GLADTITHINGS
(glad 'ty things)

Relief felt by clerks, bishops, and their wives at the end of the year when tithing settlement is finally over.

GOSPECULATE
(gaw 'spek yu layt)

The act of speculating about possible ward division, new ward leadership, or boundary changes.

HEADYWEIGHT
('hed ee 'wayt)

Fatigue of the neck after supporting sixteen heavy hands during a setting apart or a blessing.

HILARAHYMNIAC
('hil ayr uh 'him nee ak)

The charmingly funny child who innocently steals the show whenever the Primary chorus sings in sacrament meeting.

HOOPOUFLAGE
('hoop uh 'flahj)

The attempt to disguise basketball hoops by decorating them for parties or wedding receptions.

HUSBANDONED
(huz 'ban duhnd)

A wife's being left to get a family ready for church while her husband attends early meetings.

HUSHITATION
('hush i 'tay shun)

The silence during testimony meeting when everyone is secretly waiting for somebody else to stand first.

HYMNBARRASSED
(him 'bayr uhst)

When someone holds the last note of the hymn too long, or when he begins singing a fourth verse after the chorister has stopped on the third.

HYMNASIUM
(him 'nay zee uhm)

Turning the hymnbook holders into baskets for tossing rolled-up bits of paper into.

HYMNAUSEA
(him 'naw zee uh)

Sitting within audible distance of the tone-deaf member of the ward.

HYMNELBOW
(him 'el boh)

The physical infirmity developed from holding up a hymnbook for more than three verses.

IMPLAQUETICAL
(im 'plak ti kuhl)

The family home evening responsibility chart that everyone makes and no one uses.

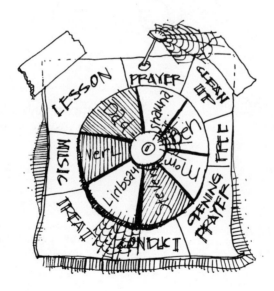

INSAMESIGN
(in 'saym 'syn)

The mistake of not listening and habitually raising your hand during sustainings—even when the bishop says, "Any opposed?"

INSEMNIA
(in 'sem nee uh)

Not being able to sleep in seminary because the teacher keeps raising his voice.

INVISAGLANCE
(in 'vis uh 'glans)

Students' deliberate looking around at the end of a lesson in an effort to avoid the teacher's eye as he selects someone to offer the closing prayer.

ISAIAHDELAYA
(iy 'zay uh dee 'lay uh)

The temptation to procrastinate that challenges any reader trying to get all the way through 2 Nephi.

ITINERWEARY
(iy 'tin uhr 'weer ee)

The feeling you get while viewing yet another returned missionary's slides. (*See also* Kodakattack.)

JOHNDICE
('jawn dis)

The sick feeling a missionary gets upon receiving a certain dreaded letter. (If the missionary is serving in Germany, the sickness is called DERjohndice.)

JOSEPHOBIA
('joh zuh 'foh bee uh)

The fear Primary-aged males experience around Christmastime, knowing that one of them will have to stand next to a girl during the manger scene.

KINDEBRIS
('kin duh 'bree)

The mess that is left around your bench as you leave sacrament meeting to take your kids to Primary.

KING SOULAMEN
(king 'sohl ay 'men)

The ward member who gives such a hearty amen that it is heard throughout the chapel.

KODAKATTACK
('koh dak uh 'tak)

A sudden, irrepressible urge to pull out the old missionary pictures and show them to visitors. (*See also* Itinerweary.)

LAZEREYE
('lay zuhr 'iy)

The unpleasant beam directed from parents in the choir toward their misbehaving children in the congregation.

LENGTHEN OR SHORTEN YOUR STRIDE
('length uhn ohr 'short uhn 'yohr 'stryd)

Adjustable pacing required during the final verse of the closing hymn for one to arrive at the podium just in time to offer the benediction.

M-LINE
('em lyn)

When a receding hairline begins to resemble the letter M, as in RM.

MANIFASTATIONS
('man i fast 'ay shunz)

Audible growling of stomachs throughout fast and testimony meeting.

MATCHELOR (MATCHELORETTE)
('mach uh lohr, or 'mach uh lohr 'et)

The eligible RM that everyone wants to "line up" with the perfect mate.

MENTALITY
('men 'tal uh tee)

Increased anxiety of a Young Single Adult woman who will soon join the Single Adult program—when her favorite hymn becomes "The World Has Need of Willing Men."

MILLENAHYMN
(mil 'en uh 'him)

When an overzealous chorister requires the congregation to sing every verse of a hymn, including the ones typed below the music.

MISDEMEANIT
('mis duh 'meen uht)

Inviting everyone to a missionary open house with the phrase, "I know we're not supposed to do this but . . ."

MTzzzzzz
('em 'tee 'zeez)

The sensation a missionary experiences after twelve hours of straight study in cubical classrooms at the Missionary Training Center.

NEPHIGHT
('nee fyt)

When knees begin to shake uncontrollably while giving a talk or solo in church.

NOCTURNAL RECOMMENDITIS
*(nawk 'tuhr nuhl
'rek uh 'men 'dy tis)*

Acute fatigue suffered by bishops, caused by issuing temple recommends at midnight to forgetful travelers, bashful brides, and misplaced missionaries.

NOLARM
('noh lawrm)

Showing up late to church on the day of a time change.

NO-UNCLEAN-FLING
('noh uhn 'kleen 'fling)

A mad dash to clean the house before visiting teachers arrive.

OOPSKIE
('oop skee)

Calling someone "Brother" or "Sister" in an out-of-church setting.

ORIGRAMI
('ohr i 'gram ee)

Meaningless folding of the program during a wearisome speaker's talk.

ORATION-SENSATION
(ohr 'ay shun sen 'say shun)

The last-minute nervousness one feels before giving a talk in church.

OVERGLOW
('oh vuhr gloh)

Reflection on the face of the speaker as the bishop flashes the little red warning light on the podium.

OVERHERD
(oh vuhr 'huhrd)

Hearing the question often asked of large LDS families, "Are all these children yours?" or the comment, "Do you think all those children belong to them?"

PANDAPHONIUM
(pan duh 'foh nee uhm)

Mad rush to be the first to call and tell the rest of the ward about a long-awaited birth or mission call.

PASTAOVER
('paw stuh oh vuhr)

The untouched Italian salad at the ward dinner.

PATRIART
('pay tree awrt)

The father who can make a winning pinewood derby car look as though it were made by a nine-year-old.

PENNIANTICS
('pen ee 'an tiks)

When the bishop's coat pocket starts to sag with coin-filled tithing envelopes from children.

PEWLOCKED
('pyu lawkt)

Being trapped at both ends of the row behind people stopping to visit.

PEWPLEGIC
(pyu 'plee jik)

The member whose legs have temporarily lost circulation from sitting on church benches.

PHONUSPRO-LIFICUS
('foh nuhs proh 'li fi kuhs)

Excess ringing of the telephone, especially noted in bishops' and Relief Society presidents' homes.

PINCHOUT
('pinch owt)

When an older child tries to make a little brother or sister cry so he can have an excuse to leave the meeting.

PINTATHALON
(pin 'ta thuh lon)

The Herculean ordeal of a Scout trying to close the clasp of the miniature award he pins on his mother's lapel.

PODAGONE
('poh duh gawn)

When the bishop presses the automatic podium-adjustment switch the wrong way and you disappear. (Not to be confused with Podagrow: The sensation experienced as the bishop lowers the automatic podium and you grow six inches.)

PODUMPTY
(poh 'dump tee)

The small misstep on the way down the stairs from the stand during a testimony meeting.

PRAYERATHON
('prayr uh 'thawn)

A benediction that goes on and on and on.

PREPRAYERED
(pree 'prayrd)

When the person giving the opening prayer spends the whole opening hymn planning what to say.

PRIMEWARY
('prym wayr ee)

Anxiety felt when you know there is an opening in the Primary organization and the bishop says he wants to meet with you after church.

PROGRAMAJAM
(proh 'gram uh 'jam)

When the greeter passing out programs can't keep up, and everyone is backed into the foyer.

PUPULAR
('puhp yu luhr)

The way missionaries feel when they find more angry dogs than investigators at home.

QUICKSIT
('kwik sit)

When you enter the chapel a little late only to realize that the person who is about to say the prayer is waiting for you to find a place.

QUILTAGABBLE
('kwilt uh 'gabl)

Small talk that occurs around a Relief Society quilting frame.

RM-BER
(awr 'em buhr)

The disconcerting feeling a returned missionary experiences when someone asks him where a scripture is found and he doesn't recall.

R-WAITED
(awr 'way tuhd)

When an otherwise good R-rated movie is censored and shown on TV.

REWARDED
(ree 'wohr duhd)

The point at which a person finally accepts a new ward as his own and stops saying, "In our old ward . . ."

REBELINT
('reh buhl int)

Persistent specks on a dark Sunday suit.

RECHOIRED
(ree 'kwy uhrd)

When you are released as the Primary chorister and are immediately called as stake music specialist.

RIPLEYASTICS
('rip lee 'as tiks)

Unbelievable calls made by church referees.

SACED-OUT
('sakd 'owt)

The condition of not being able to stay awake during sacrament meeting. (*See also* Somiknocks.)

SACRAFACIAL
('sak ruh 'fay shuhl)

The night you give up to attend a cosmetic demonstration or gift party given by a friend in the ward.

SACROSYLUM
('sak roh 'sy luhm)

The bench where the wife of a bishopric member sits alone with her young family during sacrament meeting.

SCARS AND STRIPES FOREVER
('skawrz and 'striyps fohr 'ev uhr)

Inevitable disagreements that sometimes flare during family home evening—when "Battle Hymn of the Republic" should have been the opening song.

SCRIPTHESIVE
(skrip 'tee siv)

Mysterious force that holds scripture pages together.

SCRIPZOPHRENIA
('skrip zoh 'free nee uh)

When you have a scripture in mind but cannot find it anywhere.

47

SHIVERENCE
('shi vuhr uhns)

Sitting through sacrament meeting when the church furnace has broken down again.

SHOULDER TO THE HEEL
('shohl duhr 'too thuh 'heel)

The anatomical area most painful to the fifty-year-old man still trying to play church sports.

SHOWBURRR
('shou buhr)

When everyone is rushing to get ready on Sunday morning, and you end up in the bathroom after the hot water is gone.

SHUG
(shuhg)

The awkwardness of two old mission friends meeting—one ready to shake hands, the other prepared to hug, and both quickly reversing.

SKREEL
(skreel)

Occasional high-pitched blast from the chapel microphone.

SLURCH
(sluhrch)

The hunched position of elbows on knees that young men on church benches often take. (*See also* Evidents.)

SMILEAGE
('smy lij)

Miles that build up on the family car going to and from church.

SMOTHER
('smuh thuhr)

The mom who covers her crying child's mouth during sacrament meeting.

SMUCKLE
('smuh kuhl)

When the whole congregation laughs, and the speaker doesn't know what he said that was so funny.

SNAPSPOT
('snap spawt)

The place in front of the world map at the MTC that has been captured forever in every missionary photo album.

SNOOZELETTER
('snooz letr)

The ward newspaper that is widely distributed but rarely read.

SOFTBRAWLS
('sawft 'brawlz)

Sudden disputes that occasionally break out during church athletic events.

SOMIKNOCKS
('saw mi nawks)

Little nudges to awaken nodding neighbors during meetings. (*See also* Saced-out.)

SOPHISTISPATION
(soh 'fis tih 'spay shun)

A teenager's trick of leaving a gap on a church bench between the rest of the family and himself in an effort to be disassociated from noisy brothers and sisters.

SPIFE
(spyf)

The one kitchen utensil that doesn't match any others in the meetinghouse kitchen drawer.

SQUENCH
(skwench)

Condition that results when six people squeeze onto a five-person pew.

STANDARD-FOURPLEX
*('stan duhrd
'fohr plex)*

The distress felt when a scripture reference is given and you don't know whether to search in the Book of Mormon or the Old Testament.

STATISTI-CALL
(stuh 'tis ti 'kawl)

When the bishop says your time has come to serve as a clerk.

SUNBEAMING
('suhn bee ming)

The look on proud parents' faces when their child performs a part on the Primary program.

SUNSTORM
('suhn 'storm)

A hyperactive Sunbeam.

SUPERSILLYUS
('soo puhr 'sil ee uhs)

Reduced church attendance on Super Bowl Sunday.

SWALLUMP
('swawl uhmp)

The feeling you have when the bishop announces he will be calling someone out of the congregation for an impromptu testimony.

TAMPERTATION
('tam puhr 'tay shun)

A strong desire to open a mission call envelope before the missionary gets home to open it.

TEMPORAL- PHENALIA
('tem pohr 'uhl fen 'ay lee uh)

Items missionaries end up having to send home from the MTC: books, tapes, posters, water skis, etc.

THIRSTAFELIAC
(thuhrst uh 'fi lee ak)

The child who regularly wants to leave a meeting to "get a drink." (*See also* Fountologist.)

THIRTY-FIRSTRATION
('thir tee fir 'stray shun)

The feeling you have when your home teachers make their visit on the thirty-first of every month, whether the month has thirty-one days or not.

THREEBELLION
(three 'bel yun)

When the Sunday School teacher won't stop on the first or even the second bell.

TIP-OFFS
('tip awfs)

Hints that home teachers and missionaries give to get families they are visiting to turn off the TV.

TIPTOWADDLE
('tip toh 'wawdl)

The interesting walk of members who cross the cultural hall floor so that the sound of their shoes won't disrupt any meetings. (*See also* Ashoestics.)

TOYANOYIA
('toy uh 'noy uh)

When the child in front of you in sacrament meeting drops his toy and you pick it up, and he drops it again and you pick it up, and he drops it again . . .

TRIXED-OFF
('trixt awf)

The disgruntlement felt by young parents when they arrive at church and realize the cold cereal container was never put into the diaper bag.

TROOPGOOP
('troop goop)

The food that Scouts have to cook but cannot bring themselves to eat.

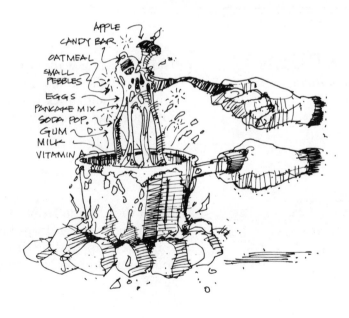

UNICALL
('yu ni cawl)

The once-a-year call for anyone with a ward sports uniform to please bring it back.

VAN GOGHHERE
('van goh 'heer)

The extra parking place created beyond the row of marked spots at a church conference or a BYU game by a driver you would like to hang up by his ears.

VEHICLE AND MR. HIDE
('vee hikl and 'mis tuhr 'hyd)

The game of owning a truck but not letting anyone know for fear it will be borrowed every moving day.

VEILCORDIANS
(vayl 'kohr dee 'uhnz)

Sliding doors in churches that transform one regular-sized room into three miniature ones.

VIDEOBEDIENT
('vi dee oh 'bee dee uhnt)

Using your VCR for nothing worse than a PG movie.

WALLWEEDS
('wawl weedz)

The young men at a church dance who stand around the sides of the cultural hall refusing to ask any girls to dance.

WASPNOSIS
(wawsp 'noh suhs)

Unified movement of the congregations' eyes when there is an insect flying in the chapel.

WEEWAHS
('wee wawz)

Newborn cries heard over the microphone during the blessing of a baby. (*See also* Blessabye.)

WHISPRAYER
('wis prayr)

The Primary president's whispering every word of a prayer in a child's ear.

WHOZEE
('hoo 'zee)

The expression on the face of a bishop's child upon seeing his father after too many meetings.

WITH WANDERING AWF
(with 'wawn dring 'awf)

A child who regularly wanders up and down the aisle during sacrament meeting.

XEROX IN THE MIRE
('zee rawks in the 'myr)

When the copy machine at the church is broken and you know you shouldn't go anywhere else to make copies because it is Sunday.

YEASOBS
('yay sawbs)

Sounds made by devout girlfriends on hearing of their boyfriends' mission calls.

ZEESRUN
('zeez ruhn)

Mad dash to the supermarket for the napkins no one brought to the ward dinner.

ZLIP
(zlip)

The inevitable last-minute run in your last pair of hose on Sunday morning.

ABOUT THE AUTHORS

It has been said that comics say funny things and comedians say things funny.
We suppose that makes Brad a sixth-grade teacher and Clark a real estate broker.

Both these young authors have seen the world — from Japan, where Clark
served his mission, to Chile, where Brad served. The world has seen Brad and
Clark — for instance, in productions such as the musical *My Turn on Earth* and the
movie *Rocky IV*. Popular speakers throughout the Church, Brad and Clark have
worked together in the BYU Outreach, Especially for Youth, and Education Week
programs.

At 6 feet 6 inches, Clark played Cougar basketball during his college years at
BYU. He is as yet unmarried. Brad, author or co-author of four books, had his first
book published by Bookcraft when he was eighteen. He has also been published
in Church magazines and *Reader's Digest*. He and his wife, Debi, have two
children. Brad lives in Provo, Utah, Clark in San Jose, California.